"I consider Philip Begho's writing of superior quality."

– Prof. Dapo Adelugba
World-renowned theater scholar

PHILIP BEGHO is the author of several award-winning books. His wide-ranging interest has seen him in a varied career that has spanned journalism, banking, business, legal practice and university teaching. He has also engaged in film and theatrical production.

He now works as a full-time writer.

By the same author

- *Songbird*
- *Strange World*
- *Jelly Baby*

- *Esther*
- *Job's Wife*
- *Joseph*
- *Jael*
- *Daniel*
- *Jephthah's Daughter*
- *Nebuchadnezzar*

- *Solomon*
- *Born King*
- *Titi Rella*
- *Leopard Woman*
- *Predator*
- *Smallie*

- *Aunty Felicia*
- *Aunty Felicia Returns*
- *Aunty Felicia in Yankari*
- *Aunty Felicia Goes to School*
- *Aunty Felicia in the Evil Forest*

- *King Omatosan*
- *Chuma the Terror*
- *Traffic Jam Kids*

TULIP OF THE NILE

PHILIP BEGHO

Monarch Books

TULIP OF THE NILE

First Published 2003

copyright © **Philip Begho** 2003
All rights reserved

All rights reserved. No part of this publication may be reproduced, stored in a retrieval system, or transmitted in any form or by means, electronic, mechanical, photo-copying, recording, or otherwise, without the prior written permission of the author or publisher, with the exception of brief excerpts in magazines, articles, reviews, etc.

Email: monarch_books@yahoo.com
Tel: +234 8060069597

ISBN 978-32224-7-3

PUBLISHED BY MONARCH BOOKS
NIGERIA

CONTENTS

BOOK ONE
(Thoughts Like Wings)

Like A Waiter	9
Wonders	10
Caesar	11
Smitten	12
Chaste Grace	13
Caged	14
Oh, For Freedom!	15
When My Way Is Dark	16
All Grace	17
Your Hands	18
Secret of the Hawks	19
Only In My Heart	20
Living Water	21
Captive	22
Truth	23
When Tomorrow Comes	24
All My Life	25
Your Dreams	26

Dreamers of Dreams	27
Paradox Vanity	28
Lycidov	29
How Deep The Night	33
Pride	34
The True Noble	35
Survival	36
Catch That Song!	37
Nor This, Adlestrop (But Zaki-Biam)	39

BOOK TWO
(Remembering the Children)

Pernickety, Pernickety!	41
Take This Song	42
Sleepy Head	44
Toffee Game	45

BOOK THREE
(Ode to the Thespian)

Lament of the Fair-Weather Wife	47
Job's Plague	49
Out of Season	50
Calamity's Instruction	51
The Affliction of the Righteous	52

Prince of Dissemblance	53
Prince of Bloodletting	54
True & False	55
True	56
Indeed	57
True Allegiance	58
Royal Grief	59
She	61
He	63
Rebellion	65
Justice & Mercy	66
By Sweet Words Felled	68
Virgin Swoop	69
Mordecai's Lament	70
Logic Unseen	71
The Fool's Song	72
At First & Then	73
My Precious!	74
Doomed?	75
Alone… But Wait…!	77
Found At Last	78

BOOK ONE
thoughts like wings

Like a Waiter

Halcyon days
Days of bliss
Whispers caught in a drifting cloud
Petals at dawn softly weeping

And time stood still like a waiter

Wonders

This flower
I plucked from the heart of silence
Between the walls of barren echoes
When it seemed the womb bore no fruit

This flower
       I plucked
              is fairer than all else
And in its heart
            is hidden
                      a harvest

   of
wonders

Caesar

How did you feel
When they said you looked like Caesar?

And one of them said,
"Lest like you, I too
Begin to look like mine,
I don't keep dogs."

Smitten

Far country of fancy and forever,
Kingdom of silver dreams and aery heather,
Sweet imagination's starry abode,
Unveil! and show to me your rainbow road.

A smitten child, star-struck, I sought you out
In pulp and celluloid mags strewn about,
Staring at faces and thinking to find
In pose of stars your rich and ranging mind.

Far country of fancy and forever!
Liquid realm! Region of streaming silver!
Imagination's jeweled coronet!—
Uncover your way! Rip this veiling net!

In adolescence, sweet as frankincense,
Still I sought you, desire now intense;
But God showed how idle was my longing,
For longing bereft of wings is nothing.

I turned, and now I fly to Morning Side,
Plumed in poesy found in Him my guide.
In yon happy heights, rainbow gates I see,
And to them I say, "Doors, yield now for me."

Chaste Grace

Panther, black panther of the night,
On velvet paws departing past,
One with the night in prowl or flight,
Can your grace compare with hers?

Swan of the graceful shades, sable swan,
In brook or pool a peerless charm,
Striking in beauty, though forlorn,
Can your grace compare with hers?

Tulip of the Nile, dark and proud,
With bell and sway to charm the air,
Rare to find, like the desert cloud,
Can your grace compare with hers?

Gazelle, pride of sea-grass Afric,
Sweet savannah's heartbreaking sight,
Chic in flight, in repose as chic,
Can your grace compare with hers?

She walks in grace, in grace abides,
Her heart and gait serene and chaste,
No finer carriage beauty rides,
Than the equipage of chaste grace.

Caged
(from *Songbird*)

Bird in a cage, how so forlorn you are!
Your eyes are sad,
They are worn and weary with weeping.

Bird in a cage, how so silent you are!
Your throat is still,
It's chained and fettered with pining.

Bird in a cage, Songbird, my Songbird!
I know your pain, your ache, your shame—
For you and I are lame.

Bird in a cage, caged bird, my caged bird!
I know your heart, your harm, your hurt—
For you and I are caught.

Oh, For Freedom!
(from *Songbird*)

Bird on the wing, how you rise in freedom!
The world is yours,
You deafen the morning with song!

Bird on the wing, what liberty you know!
Your world is wide,
You garland the heavens with joy!

Bird on the wing, Songbird, my Songbird!
Oh for your wings, your flight, your span—
But here I am enchained.

Bird on the wing, freed bird, my freed bird!
Oh for your song, your trill, your thrill—
But who will set me free?

When My Way Is Dark

When my way is dark, steeped with grief,
And no word or help brings me relief,
And my grieving depths wail, "Give up!"
I'll brace my heart, I won't give up.

When my way is dark, deep with gloom,
And each step I take seems forged for doom,
And the night around screams, "Give up!"
I'll hold my ground, I won't give up.

When my way is dark, filled with fear,
And the hunting hounds are drawing near,
And dread cries, "What's the use? Give up!"
I'll hasten on, I won't give up.

When my way is dark, dragon dark,
And I'm bludgeoned, thrown to the rack,
And darkness calls, "Give up! Give up!"
I'll spring right up, I won't give up.

I won't give up, I won't give up!
Come night or hound or dragon dread,
For once He spoke and twice I heard:
"A crown awaits; don't you give up!"

All Grace

Bad times never last for ever,
Nor seasons freeze and hold their stay,
Nature's rule as though to sever—
But cheerless clouds must fade away.

Though the night rears huge and hideous,
Though sorrow's teeth bites to the bone,
Morning's flame will burn more precious
To crop the jewel from the stone.

Though sunk in anguish, tempest tossed,
Dismayed, bereaved, and trouble-worn,
Cheer up, beloved, not all is lost;
Just trust in Him of maiden born.

He who walked upon the water,
Who spoke peace, bid the storm be still,
Waits only to hear you utter
Your trust in Him, your store to fill.

Find then in your granary all grace
To bear the storm, endure the night,
And so with joy complete the race
And rest in victory's crowning light.

Your Hands

At the Dead Sea
You stopped
And showed me your hands—

Smaller than the skies
At first they seemed

Until I looked again

Secret of the Hawks

He gazes at the hawks all day
Cresting, circling, and veering away.
His mind is latched on regions high,
His longings betrayed by a sigh.

Around him a curious world stares,
Wondering what a man besieged with cares
Should find in kites soaring above
In circled search for chick or dove.

And still he stands gazing, faithful
To a pursuit so very wasteful—
Or so it seems. But, say, what use
Can this produce, this eye's abuse?

Proud hawks, what secrets in you lie
To win you this fawn and hub of eye?
Pray, sir, tell why you stand and gaze
At birds with not a plume to daze—

Just cresting and circling all day
What beauty or dark secrets have they?
He turns. 'A man sees not,' he says,
'But the thoughts of his mind always.'

Only In My Heart

Magdalene,
Why do you weep?
You saw Him seven times, and then again;
I, on the stretch of two thousand years,

See Him only in my heart.

Living Water

The aching wind
Searches for the sea's breast
In my depths...

It will not find it there

It will find only rivers of living water

Captive

When Captivity was taken captive
Zeus himself
At the feet of Jesus Adonai

Fell

In shackles

Eternal

Truth

Truth
Has wings
That beat

In the heart
Of whom
It chooses.

How else could Cephas have known?

                How

Across years like infinity

                Do I

Across voids like eternity

                Know?

Truth
Has wings

That gather
Its own.

When Tomorrow Comes

Beloved,
Move your head,
Let me not mistakenly kiss your lips.
Give me your brow, only your brow;
When tomorrow comes

The Son must find us chaste

All My Life

Beloved,
Where have you been all my life?
I've been waiting for you
For three minutes now; *three minutes—*
And it seemed like my whole life again

Before He made us one

Your Dreams

Why
Do you let your dreams
So easily
Die?

Why
In the garden pool
Do your feet flounder
When into the sun
Your wings should soar?

You
Who in Him
Can do all things

Why
Do you let your dreams
So easily
Die?

He will bow the heavens
For you
Just for you

Why then
Do you let your dreams
So easily
Die?

Dreamers of Dreams

Surround me ever with dreamers of dreams
Vast, monumental, and unperishing,
For from such stuff
Is all that is useful to man
Formed.

Paradox Vanity

Find a man apace
There at heels vanity lopes;
Our every striving step
Is but sprung and dogged
By vain and fulsome pride.
Should we then cease to strive?
We live, then, no more.

O paradox vanity!
Proud toppler of kings,
Swift plummet of angels,
Man's first hedge from light,
Golgotha's driving nail;
Of every deed amiss, chief architect;
Initiator of every wrongful act;
And no less author, where, by absence,
The fields of deeds and acts
Lie strewn with lack.

Lycidov

I Wept not a tear for Lycidov,
Cut down and slain on the fields of self-love.
Not that I judged my friend — only God may,
But not a tear could my eyes find that day,
The day that Lycidov died. Lycidov!—
Lion-maned man with gentle heart of dove.

Poesy indeed bruised you, Lycidov,
But the mortal wound was struck by self-love,
For you had such gifts, what couldn't they do?
They charmed the world, but alas, charmed you too.
It is ever so: men's cheers bring in tow
Applause of self, which kills before you know.

O Lycidov! I couldn't weep, sweet friend,
The day you fell; no tear could I pretend.
And it was not for judging you, I say—
How could I, who once like you woke the day
With minstrelsies at the shrine of self-love,
Worshiping the gifts, not the One above.

And in you were the gifts I most preferred,
So no adulation for you was spared.
The circlet of intellect hugged your brow,
Hot like gold, yet art in you did not bow
To reason's blaze, but threw her fire too,
And flame in sweet flame, what couldn't you do?

Was any uncharmed? Was anybody?
Your thoughts were songs aflame, whose melody
Could giddy the songbird off her perch;

As for your rhymes, you had no need to search:
They teemed mint-fresh in dizzying splendor
All golden, all charming, winged with humor.

The arts and sciences, philosophy,
Sweet inventiveness, all was your trophy,
Yet it was your verses that spellbound me;
How so rapturously your rhymes winged free!
How in the sunlight they sang with glad notes,
Natural and true, fulfilling all boasts!

But you never published — you had no need:
Your life was there, you said, for all to read;
And how sweet a poem your life, how tragic!
You left, but your notes linger like music,
Like the glow of evening's exhalations,
You who could have enchanted the nations.

And I stood in the thraldom of your spell,
Trussed for the slaughter, awaiting the knell,
For this worship, I knew, bore with it death,
But what could I do, who could give me breath,
Caught and choking in idolatory's grip,
With sly Pillage taking all it could strip.

No, dear Lycidov, it was not for this
That I did not weep. Though I was remiss,
It was not for heaping on you the grief
Of my dark years, the years before relief;
No, the false worship was mine, mine the price,
Rock-ordained, not the whim of falling dice.

And even so, the price, like all else, pales

In the wondrous recall of freedom's gales
Bursting upon me, around me, in me,
Through me, with a joy mighty like the sea!
How sweet my freedom, unbearably sweet!
How great my joy, undiscoverably great!

And in my joy, Lycid, I called to you,
Beckoned you to come, but what did you do?
You clasped the shackles fallen at my feet,
Bewailing your broken spells, your defeat,
And with no eyes for the sun about me,
You stalked from the light, nighted with envy.

And still I called; you were my friend, I called!
Why should sweet salvation, my joy, be walled
By a hedge of sorrow — I be taken
But you be cast off with the forsaken?
See all I did to help — what was missing?
Oh friend, I tried but you wouldn't listen!

To come, you said, would be to surrender
Your gifts and powers; would be to tender
And exchange authority and kingship
For servitude and weak discipleship.
No! King Lycidov would bow to no one!
You strode away, glowering in the sun.

And I stood benumbed, iced with fear for you,
For you had elected self, and death too.
And when it came, when death grew to ripening,
I did not weep, Lycid, not from judging,
But because my heart raged strong against you:
If you had come, you would have lived, I knew.

And so for four hundred days and an age
I bore the burden of my mammoth rage,
My thoughts abrasive like rubble uncleared,
My heart heavy, stone-forged, with tears unshed.
But today, Lycid, I cried for you, friend;
Release came, and babe-like I cried no end:

>Sweetest friend!
>Dearest Lycidov!
>My Lycid!

How Deep the Night

You who renounce the light,
How deep
Is the night of your understanding!
You see only
What night would have you see

You peeped behind the veil
And beheld the face of night,
And wept at dawn
For what you had seen

No one told you not to peep

    Did no one tell you too
    It was no one's fault?

Pride

Pride makes foolish a clever man,
And of intelligence makes sport,
A clown, a jesting thing to scan
From the galleries on mockery's fort.

Yes, pride so quickly robs a man
Of stores of wisdom and good sense,
And like gall, does all it can
To staunch and poison his essence.

See pride yonder, digging a hole;
Conceit is close by with the staves;
Laying the net is vanity's role;
What wicked snares they set their slaves!

Beware pride, beware its faking;
Though disguised in righteous anger,
Though the mien of honor aping,
Look closely and find pride under.

Dear Lord, break now the chains of pride
That bind us to pain and ill-deeds,
And let not temperance from us hide,
But summon her to show her creeds.

The True Noble

To be noble, what must one do?
Do all that is right, and be true
To God and conscience all your days:
Honesty, even today, pays.

To be noble, how must one stand?
Stand Rock-fast, unswayed by the band
Of false mores and falser fashions
And norms alluring, which truth shuns.

To be noble face life with poise
And fear not adversity's voice;
Greet failure with cool dignity
And hurt with equanimity.

To be noble, what must one bear?
Bear all that wisdom says to bear,
And bear the lash of the tempest,
For after the storm comes life's best—

Success and joy, glad peace and rest
Mark ever the end of the test,
For those who hold the Rock to breast—
The true noble, brightest and best.

Survival

Survival, gnome and man's deceiving troll,
Defense and excuse of the private soul
As it bends aslant to escape the pain
That breathes life, would be dew and cleansing rain.
Survival, the plea of public conscience
Gone truant, shed of wisdom and good sense.

Left on your own, you belched out the jackboot,
A tribe formed and trained to subdue and loot
The target of war; and who was target
But you, dear land! You who should have been kept
Apple of the eye, petted and nestled,
Became foe, to the ground kicked and wrestled.

And so a nation was thrown to its knees,
The wine drunk to its skin and very lees—
Citrus collapsed, squeezed to its bitter rind;
And we huffed and puffed and sought the fiend,
But found only the beast — his name Survival,
His abode our hearts, sunk in graft, hate and guile.

Oh, Survival! Shame, Survival! Oh, shame!

> But arise, new Nation!
> Arise Nigeria, born anew! Arise!

Catch That Song

Catch that song that was your childhood,
Your dreams then were swan-wings unbroken in the sun.

All afternoon I stood by yesterday's light
    to fan the embers
Of yesterday's friendship, and in the half-light,
I thought I saw you stumble in.

On your back you bore the load that came
When you let the song go. And you said:
    "The night is long, the wind aches,
    It finds no where to rest its head."
And I said, "Catch the song that cries in your heart."
But you only looked back and saw the load of years.

Catch that song that cries in your heart,
The song that lived before the time of pain and waste.
If you take your heart to your ear you will hear the
    beat
Of dawn winging away from the sides of night.
If you take your heart to your ear, you will hear the
    silence
Of the sea waiting breathless for the aching wind.

You will hear, if you take your heart to your ear,
The secret of this our second life
Billowing in sails that bleed; the prows bleed,
The rudders bleed: it is finished.
And if you seek beyond the shade,
Beyond the glade of empty years,
You will see, you will see, you will see...

You will see joy leaping among the cedars,
You will see the cedars rooted upon the Word,
You will see the Word sprouting in your heart.

There — joy in the sunlight
Dancing on the wings of childhood;
In his right hand the Word,
In his left belief, on his lips a song.
His laughter gladdens the sun,
And he tires not as he beckons to all.
"Take me," he says. "I, the believing heart
Of childhood; I open up the Word, give freedom,
    breathe new life."

If you take your heart to your ear and hear the song,
Hold it close and never let go.

If you take your heart to your ear...

All afternoon I stood by yesterday's light...
           And prayed.

Nor this, Adlestrop
(But Zaki-Biam)

Nor was this Adlestrop, no—
Though it was June and the heat
In waves from the platform rose
To meet the slow-approaching train.

I do not know why they stopped,
But no one came out, nor did we, the sentries,
War-worn as we were, do more than lift up tired heads.
Not a moan. No sound from mutilated bodies in
    doorways.

My eyes settle on someone. A girl, perhaps.
I would be sure if I could find all her flesh.
What keeps her still alive? The train re-starts—
Her fingers, I see, are on the pages of a book.

I know the book, but what pages are these?
What pages? Exodus? Revelation? What pages?
Suddenly I'm desperate. I need to know. I scream:
"What pages!" But slipstream, only. And stillness.

And somewhere, in another stillness, a world away,
A train would sit easy, unwontedly, meadow sweet;
And above it, circling, surely, lower, and lower,
Birds of peace. But not here. In Zaki-Biam, birds of
    prey.

BOOK TWO

remembering the little ones

Pernickety, Pernickety!

Pernickety, Pernickety!
Jump, jump, my pernickety soul!
Rickety-ree, rickety-dee,
Lay the table, set it just so!
Quick! Fetch the spoons! When mother wakes,
She must find everything in place!

Pernickety, Pernickety!
Jump, jump, my pernickety soul!
Rickety-ree, rickety-dee,
Wash that pan, that pot, that bowl!
Quick! Wipe that plate! Where's the napkin?
Mother must find everything clean!

Pernickety, Pernickety!
Jump, jump, my pernickety soul!
Rickety-ree, rickety-dee,
How I wish dear mother knew
How I long to go and play,
But I must work, alas, all day!

Take This Song

Take this song along with you
Let it greet you at the break of dawn
To fill your heart with the morning sun

Let it greet you again at noon
And ever by dark or light of moon

Let it dance this day in your heart
And tomorrow be there and never part

And if sometime you stumble
In this place where many fumble

Or you think it's now the end
Because it's gone, your joy and hope

Don't fret, my precious friend,
Or think you cannot cope

Just listen to the beat
Of the song, 'twill ease the heat

It's a song of ancient love
The greatest love of all
Of Him who Was and Is
Who died and rose again
That you may live, and I,
In the hallowed palm of God.

"Come, beloved child,

You whom my soul has loved;
I, your King and Prince of Peace,
Am calling you today;
Let me be your light, your star,
Your heart's loving guide
To lead you through life's fitful paths
This day and evermore."

Sleepy Head

Scribble, scribble, scribble!
Clever children, scribble!
Cross your T's and dot your I's,
And don't tell any lies
When I ask dear Dozy Wize,
Why sleep confounds your eyes!

Toffee Game

Innie, minnie, clacky cluck!
There's a sweet in there to suck,
But only if I have the luck
To tell what skinny fist to rock.

Rock!

Second chance, second chance,
I dance and prance, and I'm so kind.
Second chance, second chance,
Choose me right, or we'll catch and fight.

Choose!

Innie, minnie, dicky drake,
How I need a happy break!
Tell me now for Toffee's sake,
Tell me which skinny fist to shake.

Shake!

BOOK THREE
ode to the thespian

Lament of the Fair-Weather Wife
(from *Job's Wife*)

Oh! Oh, that I have lived to see such ruins,
Such a falling apart of my world!
Night when it is yet noon, darkness ere dusk!
My own maidservant, my own servant mocks me—
An urchin, a street orphan plucked by Job
From the slimy claim of gutterous death—
She mocks me, and all on account of Job!
Everything now mocks me because of Job:
The air, my life, the seasons, everything—
They mock me, shame me, strip me woeful
    bare,
Lift me naked aloft and hurl me down bereft!
O God, what is my sin? Where have I erred?
How offended? It was but yesterday,
A little time gone past, and the land of Uz,
Her maids and all her women-folk, envied me—
Job's wife, the one who married honor himself;
Job's wife, the favored one, who in marriage
Received the hand of righteousness, complete,
As man may have, and mortal mold display.
Job's wife, perfect hew of Eastern women
    blessed!
Riches and honor, children and love and health—
All were mine, my life was whole and rounded,
Fresh and gladsome as the air at dewy dawn,
And then the Sabeans came with thirsty swords,
And lo! the fire hurtling from heaven,
And ere the news was heard the slaughtering
    Chaldeans!
And oh — oh! — the wind across the desert

And in one day my fruit manifold gone!
Tortured day! Tortured day and season vile!
Left with one who is nor man nor husband—
A barely breathing piece of putrid flesh,
A crawling covert for maggots and flies!
What is my offense, how have I transgressed?
Once the toast of Eastern women, now the
    shame!
And all for Job! Job of Uz whom I wed—
And would not, had I but seen with prescient eye
The end and dishonor of tainted righteousness!
But no more! Today the bird escapes her snare
And, before the groaning starts, wings aloft!

    —— You would escape your husband? —

Husband? No more. May dead flesh husband a wife?

Job's Plague
(from *Job's Wife*)

See what was once living flesh and weep.
The flesh has died upon him and he lives still.
He has worms for flesh and boils for skin,
Yet breath issues from him, he would not die.
Flies wrap him as a shroud but he is no corpse.
Do you not smell the air, vile vapors abroad?
'Tis the stench from him, his flesh, his
    breath.
Can you not smell it? The air here is sick!
Defilement has pitched tent here, contagion reigns.
Yet, 'tis the groaning — oh! —I most dread.
It comes at dusk and ceases only at dawn.
All evening, through the endless night, the
    groaning.
Nothing shuts it out, nothing may quench it.
It overthrows slumber, slaughters sleep...
Oh, dreadful dragon of night, tenor dread!

Out of Season
(from *Job's Wife*)

It is the foolish wise who embrace alone
Erudition and forsake wise discernment
Which clears the clouds and reveals the seasons:
The season for debate and for restraint,
For rebuke and for repair, to chide and cheer.
Job needed balming waters from the fountains
And springs of cool comfort and consolation,
But from his friends got only smothering tar
From the wells of argument and clamor.

Calamity's Instruction
(from *Job's Wife*)

Ever alive in the corpse of calamity
Is instruction. But instruction for whom?
The smitten? Not always, or not only.
The witnesses, sometimes, are in the main
Intended to be the event's beneficiaries.
They must observe, question, interpret,
Examine their hearts: and this is prime,
Unwrap their covering garments of self- deceit,
See their soul in all its bare nakedness,
Admit its truth, learn and be instructed.
The smitten, sometimes, is merely he found
    worthy
To bear the suffering that instructs his fellows.
And for this service his reward is sure,
Unalterable, for God is a just God,
And abides no indebtedness to man.
Now from this calamity, Job's affliction,
What instruction has Job's wife uncovered?
She has learnt, I think, spousal desertion—
How to pack her bags and leave when most
    needed.
In fair weather she says, 'Let none grudge me
That I of Job's prosperity do partake:
He is my husband, his portion is mine.'
But in tempest she says, 'I must detach myself;
No flesh is no husband, my portion lies abroad.'
Job's wife is nothing but a common harlot,
The most ignoble run of fortune-seekers
Who may, with the fair-weather coin of fortune,
Be bought and sold and market-haggled.

The Affliction of the Righteous
(from *Job's Wife*)

In all the earth there was none so righteous
And so blameless before God as the man Job.
He was afflicted, not for any sin,
But to test him and all those around him.
He fell to offense only when his friends came
And scrabbled his soul to unleash bitterness.
For then in acrimony Job suggested
That God was unjust to afflict the
    righteous.
He offended there, for God is never unjust.
It is the privilege of the Lord God,
Our maker, the creator of all that is,
He who set the outposts of wisdom and knowledge,
The pillars of the rules that govern man,
In His wisdom to afflict a righteous man
In order to test him, to strengthen him,
To purify him, or to heroify him
For His glory's sake, or so that his fellows
May by his suffering be tested and schooled.

Prince of Dissemblance
(from *Daniel*)

A panther? Me, O king? The king knows
I am but a doe's innocent nursling,
A child's sweet pet, gentle in all my ways,
Soft and tender, and slow even to tread ground,
Lest, perchance, I hurt the unwary earth.

A buzzard? Me, O king? The king knows
I am but a dove's younger brother,
A bird of peace, gentle in all my ways,
Soft and tender, and slow even to draw breath,
Lest, perchance, I hurt the delicate air.

Prince of Bloodletting
(from *Daniel*)

Once at Ashkenaz, in the black belly
Of midnight's deepest rage, a mere lad,
I found a thousand ways to thrust that blade
And let out blood; warm blood, rich and bubbly.
That traitor, O king, has veins of rich blood.
Will it not please the king have me show the king,
In the belly of that man, my thousand ways?

True or False
(from *Daniel*)

The art of life is the art of compromise:
To yield and bend with the wind of expedience,
And slack off in season, and firm up with prudence;
And to give and take and share, or else withhold,
As the times command and good sense will have!

True
(from *Daniel*)

Beware expedience, O king, it is double-faced,
Of changing gait, and walks not firm with lone-faced
    truth;
And compromise dines with prudence and good sense
Only where integrity is honored guest.

Indeed
(from *Daniel*)

God is God, and man is man though he be king;
No man is king but God makes him so,
And no man gains worth but God enables.
Therefore must men, king and all, honor God.

True Allegiance
(from *Daniel*)

I fear you, O king, but I fear God more;
And I must speak as God would have me speak.
And though I'm your servant, I'm first God's
    servant,
And must love you, and serve and honor you,
Only as may honor my first allegiance.

Royal Grief
(from *Daniel*)

I cannot sleep, no. Night comes, and sleep flees.
Why has sleep plucked my peace and fled my breast?
Why am I like one bereft of choicest gift?
Who is Daniel? What is the man to me?
Was Daniel sired of my father's loins?
No! More precious by far than such a one was he
Who played the thrice-blessed role of trusted
    friend,
Able counselor, and most devoted subject.
Here was Daniel, my joy and golden promise
Of brighter tomorrows in silvered age—
And here — here! — In the bounds of this very
    here!—
Were those two unworthies and that woman,
And in the space of a shriveled evening
Daniel is no more...

And how he stood like a man before my fire!
Had I heard it told in tale or fable
I'd have held the exploit proud to my breast;
But since the deed affronts my very self,
Like a royal hypocrite, a regal two-face,
I cast the deed from me, as sup for beasts.
A blaze of kings arrayed in golden robes
Will not match the shine of Daniel's spirit,
Nor all the armor of war-proud valor
Best the iron-breast of that Jew's courage!

Daniel! Hot did your words burn and deep did they
    pierce

When you said, 'Man is man though he be king':
For I am mere man, the smallest of men,
I who cannot stifle my heart's sobbing,
Nor quench the grief within for what my hand has
    wrought:
The hand of my pride — Pride, the bane of kings,
And the snare of fools — Fool! — Fool that I am
To deny the existence of a Maker
And say no hand made me, none wrought my form!
No! I'm not so lifted with pride, so sunk in sin
I cannot see, that though I have conquered lands
And trampled the earth with hooves and chariot
    wheels,
And with the sweep of my sword and marvelous arm
Have won the homage of nations and men—
That grain of sand, the smallest in my empire,
That strand of hair, the thinnest in my kingdom—
Defies my arm and power to mold or forge.

She
(from *Daniel*)

What fools men are! Of cheap and little use
But as toys and playthings to be dangled
By scheming maids or clever matrons
On little mocking strings, and perchance played
As one may a tried lute or mastered harp.
They look far but see little beyond their nose,
For pride, like a dark veil, falls from their brow
And drapes off any seeing but what pride allows:
They look a woman's way and see not her substance
But the picture foist by vanity's conceit:
A useful dollop of obedient flesh
Molded for the pleasure of lustful loins,
The feeding of dilated egos,
Or the vapid chore of baby breeding.

Some hold them as fit only to be spurned—
As did Daniel. Yes, Daniel, you spurned me.
I gave you my heart but you had no eyes:
I was nothing to you but a little fly
Disturbing the gaze of your noble face.
Ask now for Daniel... Where is Daniel?
Daniel, where are you? Prince, noble and damned!

You stood by your God and by your God you fell,
Stung by a little fly for whom you had no face.
Ah, proud Daniel! Too proud to stoop to sin.
Your pride, though of different face, was one with the
    king's,
For pride is pride, and all pride is folly,
And destruction dogs ever the heels of the fool.

Pride has lost the king his garrison in Daniel
And pride will lose the king his very life;
For a serpent coils beneath his pillow
And must sting him to uncoil to greatness,
But vanity shows the king the flower only
That scents his pillow, not the serpent.

Satala, you too! Prince of little fools!
You share the common folly of the king's court!
So you would be king? Satala, you?
No, Satala, I, Hajitha, shall be monarch:
Ruler of all Babylon: empress of the earth:
The pride of ages! The flower of centuries!
And by my star, the stars of Sheba and Nefertiti
Shall be as the twinkle of the king's dying tears.

What fools men are! What silly little fools!

He
(from *Daniel*)

What treachery may lurk in a woman's breast!
What nameless serpents, what nests of scorpions
May live and therein thrive to deceive
And betray the companion of her voyage
And him to snare to death, or worse than death—
For there is an evil worse than the fangs of death;
'Tis the perfidy of sanctified love:
When matrimony's band uncoils a serpent
And the gold of love's bond is hissing beast
Deaf to love, and blind to all that's chaste!

Begone from me, vile hissing beast! Begone!

Oh, had I never married or wooed amiss!
Had I not married wrong and brought to breast
This sting of treachery, this perfumed snake,
Then had my life been wholesome and perfect,
For then would Daniel, my gift from heaven,
Pure, noble and able, have lived and prospered,
And in flourishing had prospered me and mine—
My house and the stretches of my dominion,
While I, in peaceful ease, lived out my years!

Though pride has been my folly, and though 'tis true
Pride has power to make men slay their loves
And do such deeds as would raise great cheers in
    hell,
This pride was of no common spark, but stoked
    ablaze
By fiendish cunning from the heart of deepest hell!

And not dismayed by nobleness of spirit,
Nor intimidated by advanced years,
She would corrupt the hoary-haired gray-beard
And defile that pillar of chastity!

Cobra top and wicked hood of deceit—
Filled with viperous evil and aspic works!
The pith and pulse of perfect perversity!

Daniel! Oh, Daniel!
In darkest night does your star shine brighter still!
Would that the God whom you feared and dreaded
Above the fear and dread of kings and death,
Had in his dreadful arm the strong power
To snatch life from death and revive dead
    bones,
And give again to his faithful servant
The gift of breath, to his obedient one,
The lease again of life, and bring you back
To a grieving king, a wretched monarch!

Rebellion
(from *Esther*)

Rebellion is but born to be crushed;
It cannot hide in royal robes and snarl.
It is rebellion though clad in silken garb;
Rebellion, consigned to the short-lived day.
Queen Vashti's deed slurs not the king
    alone
But all men, exalted or beggarly low.
It is the firebrand to kindle in women
Wicked embers of smoldering defiance.
What fate is a man's whose gate will not lock?
What fate a city's whose walls do mutiny breathe?
Let the king therefore with no leave of further
    stay
Give the law swift motion, and in iron ribs
Of terms unalterable, to where no wind
Or fancy flutters, banish the rebel queen.

Justice & Mercy
(from *Esther*)

To behold your face, O king, at close approach
Was a dream that besieged me till I found means
To slip into your banquet of favored princes.
And now that I have seen the king's face
I dread no more the yielding of this flesh
To decay, nor fear the closing of day.
Your bounty, O king, is voiced earth-wide by golden
    deeds;
Do all men not know it?
I, like prince and courtier here, with trancèd eye,
Have seen the golden depths of royal breast
And do still float in eddies of delight.
And as for the king's might, it twins his bounty:
In vassal glitter and chains of opulent thrones
Stretching the backs of sprawling nations,
Tremoring the very stars to fearful homage.
Do all men not know it?
They know it, and their hearts with wonder
    throb.
All men know the king's bounty, his awesome might,
But do all men know this thing which I, today,
In this place, with marvel-sodden eyes have seen?
For though these eyes have gazed upon the king,
Where men have seen the king, not so these eyes.
They have gazed and seen virtue's own sire,
Virtue's fount, the very spring of virtue;
And on his brow what name bears he but
    Mercy?
Mercy today has walked the onyx of these floors,
And graced this day the cedars of these walls,

And in walking his course has met Justice,
And Justice to Mercy has bowed the knee
As lesser virtue always to greater will bow.
For Justice did decree Queen Vashti's death,
But Mercy said 'Not so,' and Mercy did prevail.
O most worthy king! Who with streaming light
Of purest virtue has blazed me blind
And from my tongue wrung praise so deeply drawn
It empties its vault now of every strength
And wilts me down at Virtue's feet!

By Sweet Words felled
(from *Esther*)

Had flattery not so thickened his sight,
He would have seen it was not I who lay
In prostrate state serene, but he himself,
Fabled king of Persia, jeweled monarch
Of the opulent East, emperor enthroned
Of the conquered world, by honey-drippings
Of sweet words felled, by slick of tongue slid.
Men grown in elevation and conceit fall quick
To flattery's tripping. From my square of
    floor
I heard the happy rumble of his stomach
Disporting in the juice of my words, and I saw
What always I had known: all power to topple
Is locked in a tongue's command. Today my tongue
Has made me prince; will not the selfsame tongue
Tomorrow raise me to power's pinnacle
Where by merest words I may about my shoulders
Gather me my dream? Nor can riches or fame
Or power, or other strong desire,
Outpeak this dream.

Virgin Swoop
(from *Esther*)

Zeresh this day did I humble tradition's back
And break the yoke of the Seven. I urged,
And the king listened; could he do otherwise?
He caught my counsel to wive in manner
Not by treaty or tradition forced,
Nor by pressure pressed, but in fancy's
    sweep
To take to breast a maiden sweet and fair,
Pliant, full pleasing, unstuck by nobility's
Stony core. And because he listened,
Bowing freely to my words, Susa's air
Tingles now with secret plans to swoop
Upon the sleeping realm and gather maidens
Of virgin breath and beauty.

Mordecai's Lament
(from *Esther*)

They took her. My Esther is gone,
My Hadassah, my myrtle blossom...

Myself has done this deed. 'Find your maid her man,'
Said all, but had Mordecai ears to hear?
Filled to deafness were my ears by the beat
That holds me thralled, binds me from the homeland,
And now has bound my daughter to the court
Of cruel concubinage. Alas! Woe is me! Oh, alas!

—Be a man.—

Alas that I'm a man and no unfeeling beast!
Else who is a man? Lay here bronze for flesh
And I shall be that man of silent lips;
Or lend me sodden sense of brutish beast
And I shall be him you would have me be;
Or give me marble shard and take this heart—
But no heart grows here now: it fell — alas!—
When my myrtle blossom did fall. I am a man.
But what a man I am, who, with slaughterous hand
Of omission, has slain his very own!

Logic Unseen
(from *Esther*)

Sense and logic are but fallible servants of the mind
And must in season yield to impulse deep sprung;
But peer with me with eyes that glean the past
And tell me if I dissemble to say:
Logic unseen today, time does in time display.

The Fool's Song
(from *Esther*)

Had I sniffed my life along the path
Of barren emotions as you would have me do,
I would not now reek princely air and power.
I've raised myself to grand and lofty heights
By fixing my sights ever on gain.
Who love not profit sit reach in folly;
Who live not for gain come soon to
    pain—
As Bigthana and Terez soon will know.
Call them not 'Bigthana' and 'Terez'
But 'Folly' and 'Folly'. Had they reasoned
And asked but this: 'What gain for Haman,
Why expect Haman to hold our cause?'
Then would they not have spent garlic breath
To conscript me ally and advocate.
But let them wait and wait and sit in folly—
Haman goes nowhere for them.

At First & Then
(from *Esther*)

At First –
He would not bow; now he eats dust, snorts dirt,
And snaffles sandy ground. He grovels and gnashes,
Befogged by ashes, who once was bright with pride:
Too proud to bow to Haman.

Then –
With springy steps did I leave the queen's banquet,
My heart light and flighty as the evening air,
My thoughts soft as sweetest song—
And there he was!—
Sitting at the gate, calm as a cave,
Sure as the hills, unmoved, unmarred, unmastered!
Sight never so slew me, nor gaze galled me dead!

His sackcloth and ashes gone, his wailing ceased,
His silence damning, his face hard, flint-stone hard,
Stiff-wrapped and steep, defiant and damning!
Careless that all the world to me did fall
On cowed and bended knees! Oh! Zeresh!

Royal fête fled my breast, all joys and pleasures
    skipped!
What manner of man would scorn the breath of death?
What strong steel holds that man? On what rock
Stands he bold? What hand keeps his mountain firm?

My Precious!
(from *Esther*)

Esther, my precious! My Esther...
That I may behold my queen...
These eyes — was it not for this they hurt,
Aching to behold fair beauty's own eyes?

Wondrously arrayed with gifts of healing
Have you come, my beloved, my precious, my queen...
My heart beats soft now, 'tis whole and content;
Gentle peace lays cooling hands on my brow,
And in my eyes dew freshness sprinkles sweet
    surcease...
That the spark and charge of my distemper
Should be the channel now of my healing...

Ah, my heart, do you weep?
Wherefore do you weep? Why, Esther? Why, my
    queen?
Esther, like Esther, ever grace will mirror—
And style and poise and sweet enigma's charm!

My beloved, my fair and precious jewel,
How my soul has longed to laugh and dine with you!

Doomed?
(from *Esther*)

Great king,
At Hellespont, in youth's fair dawning,
Back to back in bloody fray, who, O king,
Stood with you when no brother would, and with battle-
 ax
And bleeding sword, did heave when you did heave,
Did strike when you did strike, smote when you smote,
Brandishing when you brandished, nor tiring once,
Nor flinching ever, till clashing steel made ringing song
Of battle's bloody air, and Persia's fainting men,
Happy always for song, fainted no more,
But resurged in thunder strokes that soon
 made
Hellen's routers Hellen's routed,
And set Persia's name striding gory proud
Into gallant history's timeless fields?
Who was it stood with you and did this thing?
Who, O king?

—You it was... who yourself threw yourself
This day into death's unhappy court.
Choose therefore your manner of dying
And shuffle verbiage no more! Choose!—

My king,
I fear not death nor flinch from night's grave call,
Yet duty so deep is in me ingrained
It has eyes to see that the king tomorrow,
When this passing malady has fled his sight,
Will say 'Would Tabriz had lived to serve me

As ever he did; to honor me
As was his happy wont. Would someone that day
Had stayed my hand!' Therefore does my duty say:
Stay your hand, O king, and render mercy;
Render mercy, O great king!

——Mercy! Had I mercy to bestow,
Think I first would not bestow it on myself?
And on my brow raise yon scepter and say,
'Quench! You burning thing! Quench! Burn not! Burn no
    more!'?
But no more! No more be said than this:
Who ventures here, who comes unbidden dies!
Nor will I ever from this word swerve,
Though himself who accosts these portals
Were mightiest Darius, that greatly revered king,
Beloved sire of mine, whose memory...
Whose memory... Oh, I care not! Nothing now is
    true!
Nothing beloved or dear! All is dry dust, dead grit!
No, not anything, nor anyone,
Will from this word sway me: Who defies me dies!
Who enters is undone!
[*Gong sounds, and the sanctum doors open.*]
What! Who?

Esther!

Alone... But Wait...!
(from *Esther*)

Dogs have their bitches, peasants their wenches,
Bond slaves their slattern maids, but your king,
Your king can find his sail nor lift nor wind.

—My king, the wind tonight shall swell the seas.—

The seas swell and swarm with legs and arms
And nectared breasts, the scented tokens
Of your happy labors; but where, harem chief,
Is the dew, the cleansing breath, I seek?

—My efforts, O king, now have filled the catching
    net.—

Your efforts have left my mind unmated,
My heart unfulfilled. These scented maids
That nightly swamp my sight with virgin wares
Spark in me no burning fire, quench no thirst.
I need more than honey, much more lasting fare.

—She stands now at the door,
She whom the king has waited for.—

Found At Last!
(from *Esther*)

'**Twas** your eyes, piercing the veil of gloom
That strange and wondrous night, that tranced me
To new perceiving: here stood my life,
And little had known it; here, the very end
Of all my waiting; the reason at last
For nuptial dilatoriness, my daffodil mind,
Those tears that ever fell to ambush all wedlock
    talk.
Drop all daggers, then said I, and walk the shine
Of love's own glint.

Oh, how sweet is love when found at last!

www.ingramcontent.com/pod-product-compliance
Lightning Source LLC
Chambersburg PA
CBHW032211040426
42449CB00005B/544